faithfulness

Other Studies in the Fruit of the Spirit Bible Study Series

faithfulness

The Foundation of True Friendship

Jacalyn Eyre

GRAND RAPIDS, MICHIGAN 49530

ZONDERVAN™

Faithfulness: The Foundation of True Friendship
Copyright © 1991, 2001 by Jacalyn Eyre
Requests for information should be addressed to:
Zondervan, *Grand Rapids, Michigan 49530*

ISBN 0-310-23863-3

Interior design by Melissa Elenbaas

Printed in the United States of America

08 09 10 /❖ CH/ 15 14 13 12 11 10

CONTENTS

FRUIT OF THE SPIRIT
BIBLE STUDIES

Welcome to Fruit of the Spirit Bible Studies. This series was written with one goal in mind—to allow the Spirit of God to use the Word of God to produce his fruit in your life.

To get the most from this series you need to understand a few basic facts:

Fruit of the Spirit Bible Studies are designed to be flexible. You can use them in your quiet times or for group discussion. They are ideal for Sunday school classes, small groups, or neighborhood Bible studies.

The eight guides in this series can be used in any order that is best for you or your group.

Because each guide contains only six studies, you can easily explore more than one fruit of the Spirit. In a Sunday school class, any two guides can be combined for a quarter (twelve weeks), or the entire series can be covered in a year.

Each study deliberately focuses on only one or two passages. That allows you to see each passage in its context, avoiding the temptation of prooftexting and the frustration of "Bible hopscotch" (jumping from verse to verse). If you would like to look up additional passages, a Bible concordance will give the most help.

The questions help you *discover* what the Bible says rather than simply *telling* you what it says. They encourage you to think and to explore options rather than to merely fill in the blanks with one-word answers.

Leader's notes are provided in the back of the guide. They show how to lead a group discussion, provide additional information on questions, and suggest ways to deal with problems that may come up in the discussion. With such helps, someone with little or no experience can lead an effective study.

SUGGESTIONS FOR INDIVIDUAL STUDY

1. Begin each study with prayer. Ask God to help you understand the passage and to apply it to your life.
2. A good modern translation, such as the *New International Version,* the *New American Standard Bible,* or the *Revised Standard Version,* will give you the most help. However, the questions in this guide are based on the *New International Version.*
3. Read and reread the passage(s). You must know what the passage says before you can understand what it means and how it applies to you.
4. Write your answers in the space provided in the study guide. This will help you to clearly express your understanding of the passage.
5. Keep a Bible dictionary handy. Use it to look up any unfamiliar words, names, or places.

SUGGESTIONS FOR GROUP STUDY

1. Come to the study prepared. Careful preparation will greatly enrich your time in group discussion.
2. Be willing to join in the discussion. The leader of the group will not be lecturing but will encourage people to discuss what they have learned in the passage. Plan to share what God has taught you in your individual study.
3. Stick to the passage being studied. Base your answers on the verses being discussed rather than on outside authorities such as commentaries or your favorite author or speaker.
4. Try to be sensitive to the other members of the group. Listen attentively when they speak, and be affirming whenever you can. This will encourage more hesitant members of the group to participate.
5. Be careful not to dominate the discussion. By all means, participate! But allow others to have equal time.
6. If you are the discussion leader, you will find additional suggestions and helpful ideas in the leader's notes at the back of the guide.

FAITHFULNESS

The Foundation of True Friendship

Where do we go from here?"

Our family had just moved to England on a limited ministry assignment. Because we would only be there a year or so, we had decided not to bring our furniture. So my husband and I and our three boys undertook our adventure with two suitcases apiece.

We were staying with colleagues while we looked for a place to live. We exhausted the ads in the newspaper. Everything seemed too small or too expensive. In a new country without familiar resources, we felt very disoriented and vulnerable.

From out of the blue, a woman stepped from the crowd at the church where we were visiting. She introduced herself as Sue and then proceeded to ask enough questions to know everything about us.

Sue then, much to our surprise, warmly offered her services. She helped us find a house, negotiate terms, connect the utilities, locate furniture, and provided transportation. Two weeks after our initial meeting we were comfortably settled in the perfect house for our family.

We continued to benefit from Sue's hospitality through our entire stay in England. There were times when we felt we asked too much and when we feared we were imposing. But we never got any such signals from our "hostess." She and her family were there to continue to welcome and receive us. The message spoken and lived was, "You can depend on us."

God values such faithful friendships. In fact, God is the source and standard of friendship. In the Old Testament, God demonstrates the meaning of faithfulness as he calls Abraham, encourages Joshua, and forgives and loves Israel.

In the New Testament, Jesus is our model of faithfulness. He is not only the Lord of the disciples but also their friend. Jesus tells them in John 15:15, "I no longer call you servants, because a servant does not know his master's business. Instead, I have called you friends."

Scripture also contains numerous examples of men and women who committed themselves to God and to each other and who became faithful friends. Joshua worked for years as a faithful friend and aid to Moses. Ruth was a faithful companion to Naomi when life seemed filled with death, failure, and hopelessness. Jonathan was the friend of David and helped him even at the cost of Saul's anger and Jonathan's own claim to the throne. Barnabas was a faithful friend to the apostle Paul and was there to sponsor him when Paul was held in suspicion by the early church.

The faithful friendships between these people in the Scriptures brought blessings beyond measure. Joshua became the general who led Israel into the Promised Land. Ruth married into the nation of Israel and became the great-grandmother of King David and part of the line leading to the Messiah. Jonathan's friendship with David opened the way for David to become the great king whose ultimate heir would be Jesus Christ. And Barnabas launched Paul into a ministry that spread the gospel through the Roman Empire.

We all need faithful friends. And just as important, we need to learn to *be* faithful in our friendships. As you work through this Fruit of the Spirit Bible study, you will discover that faithfulness includes: a commitment to be there the way Ruth was for Naomi; a willingness to forgive the way Hosea forgave his adulterous wife; a promise of support the way God supported Joshua as he led Israel; an honoring of commitments the way God required of Israel in a time of social decay; and a fulfilling of responsibilities the way Jesus taught his disciples just before his crucifixion. Finally, because faithfulness is difficult, we need to know that there are rewards for those who make the determined effort.

May God cause the fruit of faithfulness to grow in all of your relationships.

one

A COMMITMENT TO BE THERE

Ruth 1

There is an old saying that when times are hardest you know who your friends are. That summarizes the first chapter of the book of Ruth.

Naomi's situation was at its worst. She had lost her husband and sons, which meant that she had also lost her source of income, security, and identity. She was without hope. It is at this point that Ruth, her daughter-in-law, does an astonishing thing—she decides to stay with Naomi. Ruth demonstrates a commitment to be there.

Warming Up

1. Why is faithfulness an important quality in friendship?

Digging In

2.   Read Ruth 1. What do we learn about Naomi in verses 1–5?

3.   Ruth and Orpah are introduced as Naomi's daughters-in-law (v. 4). What basis do these three women have for mutual trust (vv. 1–5)?

4.   Consider a time when you shared a difficult experience with someone. How did it strengthen your friendship?

5.   What do verses 6–13 reveal about Naomi's relationship to God?

6.   When you have faced a painful experience, how has it affected your attitude toward God?

7.   The famine is over, and Naomi prepares to return to Bethlehem with her daughters-in-law. Why does Naomi encourage Ruth and Orpah to stay in Moab (vv. 8–14)?

8.   What cost does Naomi face by encouraging Ruth and Orpah to stay in Moab?

      How do both Ruth and Orpah show faithfulness to Naomi by their different responses?

9.   What does it cost you to be faithful to those you love?

10. Read Ruth's familiar words in verses 16–17. How would you summarize her words of dedication?

11. Naomi's homecoming is painful (vv. 19–22). How does Naomi view herself and her situation?

12. What provisions has God made for Naomi even in the midst of this bitter time?

13.   In what situations is it most important for us to be there for our loved ones and friends?

How does Ruth's example encourage you to be faithful in good times and in bad?

Pray about It

Our Father, teach us to recognize and understand friendship. Teach us how to receive friendship. Teach us how to be a friend. Like Naomi, give us the capacity to know, show, and speak our feelings—love, anger, longing, bitterness, despair, and devotion. Like Orpah, give us the ability to separate from those we love if it is required of us. Like Ruth, who reflects your character, give us the courage to be faithful; to give support, love, and commitment; and to cling to those you call into our lives. May we show kindness especially to those who feel judged and rejected. Father, teach us friendship. Teach us faithfulness.

TAKING THE NEXT STEP

According to *The American Heritage Dictionary of the English Language,* third edition, faithfulness is the act of "adhering firmly and devotedly, as to a person, a cause, or an idea." Synonyms are loyal, true, constant, fast, steadfast, staunch. Faithfulness suggests undeviating attachment. Close your eyes, sit quietly, and imagine yourself in a conversation with God about faithfulness. If you have any questions, ask them. Afterward, record this conversation. Spend a few moments in reflection.

List times when you have been angry with God or felt deserted by him, even judged by him. Now list ways in which God has been faithful to you. List ways you have been faithful to God. When and how did you make your first commitment to God?

Ruth's commitment to Naomi seems extreme, yet this type of commitment is often made in marriage and many times in friendships. Make a list of those who are dear to you. In times when you felt empty, how have they been faithful to you? What kindnesses have they shown you? In times when you rejoiced, who has been with you to share your celebration? In what ways have you shown faithfulness and loyalty to your friends?

Spend time in thanksgiving. Thank God for your relationship with him and for the faithfulness he has shown you. Thank him for the people he has given you to love and for their friendship.

two

A WILLINGNESS TO FORGIVE

Hosea 2:19–3:5

Shallow relationships characterize our culture. Job transfers from city to city expand our contacts but keep our roots shallow. It is easy just to think about finding new friends when we run into problems with our current ones.

God isn't like that. As we see from the book of Hosea, God makes commitments for both time and eternity. Through the faithful prophet Hosea, who reclaims his adulterous wife, God shows what lengths he is willing to go to in forgiving and being faithful to us.

Warming Up

1.   Why do you think forgiveness is one of the foundations of friendship?

Digging In

2.   Read Hosea 2:19–3:5. Looking back at 2:13, how would you describe the spiritual condition of Israel?

3.   The word *betroth* is used three times in verses 19–20. What virtues and qualities characterize this commitment?

4.   God describes Israel's restoration in terms of marriage because he views idolatry as spiritual adultery. Why do you think God uses such a graphic term?

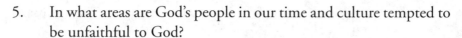

5.   In what areas are God's people in our time and culture tempted to be unfaithful to God?

In what areas do you struggle to be faithful to God?

6.   The damaged relationship between God and Israel is repaired because God is willing to forgive. How would you describe the overflowing benefits that come from this reconciled relationship (vv. 21–23)?

7.   Why can it be so difficult to forgive those who are close to us?

What overflowing benefits result when we do forgive?

8.   Verses 3:1–5 focus on Hosea and Gomer. Verse 1 tells how Gomer, though married to Hosea, is living with another man and worshiping other gods. God tells Hosea to reclaim his unfaithful wife. Given Hosea's situation, what do you think he would be thinking and feeling?

What reason does God give Hosea for this command to reclaim Gomer?

9. Hosea must pay a price to reclaim Gomer (v. 2). How does Hosea's restoration of Gomer foreshadow the ministry of Jesus Christ?

10. Forgiving love is costly. What price have you paid when forgiving another?

How does this passage motivate you to do whatever is necessary to forgive?

11.   How does this passage encourage you in your relationship to God?

Pray about It

Our Father in heaven,
hallowed be your name,
your kingdom come,
your will be done
on earth as it is in heaven.
Give us today our daily bread.
Forgive us our debts,
as we also have forgiven our debtors.
And lead us not into temptation,
but deliver us from the evil one.

—Matthew 6:9–13

TAKING THE NEXT STEP

"Get rid of all bitterness, rage and anger, brawling and slander, along with every form of malice. Be kind and compassionate to one another, forgiving each other, just as in Christ God forgave you" (Eph. 4:31–32).

Consider times when, like Gomer, you were not in the least interested in God. What "Baals" drew your attention? What riches or rewards did you seek or experience from these gods? How did God draw you to himself, and how has he blessed you? How have you experienced God's forgiveness and faithfulness?

Make a list of the costs and benefits you have experienced in the process of forgiving a friend. Include in this list those to whom you need to extend forgiveness.

As you reflect on this list move into a time of praise. Praise God for your ability to pay the cost and for the blessings that came out of that forgiveness. If you are unable to forgive, then petition God to give you the ability and grace to forgive. If this prayer is not answered quickly, be patient. You are precious in God's heart, and he is faithful. Use the fruitful, growing images God uses as he renews his commitment to Israel in Hosea 2:21–23 to thank God for his commitment to you:

> "In that day I will respond,"
> declares the LORD—
> "I will respond to the skies,
> and they will respond to the earth;
> and the earth will respond to the grain,
> the new wine and oil,
> and they will respond to Jezreel [all Israel].
> I will plant her for myself in the land;
> I will show my love to the one I called 'Not
> my loved one.'"

three

A PROMISE OF SUPPORT

Joshua 1:1–9

At our church we sing the words "Be bold, be strong, for the Lord your God is with you." My youngest son thought we were singing "Be bald, be strong. . . ."

As Joshua faced the daunting task of following Moses, I can imagine that he felt exposed and bald.

At times we all accept responsibilities that seem overwhelming. How well we perform frequently depends on the support and friendship of those around us.

In this chapter Joshua moves into a new "pastoral position" of leading over a million people. As the Lord promises to support Joshua, we observe a new facet of faithfulness and friendship.

Warming Up

1. Recall a time when you took on a project or responsibility that seemed too massive. How did you feel?

Digging In

2.   Read Joshua 1:1–9. Moses is dead. How do you think Joshua
      would have felt about becoming Israel's leader after forty years of
      Moses' leadership?

3.   As Joshua begins to lead Israel into the Promised Land, what assur-
      ances does God give him (vv. 1–5)?

4.   God promises to be with Joshua (v. 5). Why would that be
      encouraging?

5.   What difference does it make when someone offers to come with you to accomplish a hard task?

6.   What does God require of Joshua in order to be successful and prosperous in leading Israel (vv. 6–9)?

7.   Joshua must meditate on the Law day and night (v. 8). How do you think this would help him to lead Israel?

8.   How have you been supported and strengthened by a knowledge of the Scriptures?

9.   God tells Joshua not to be discouraged or terrified (v. 9). Why do you think this command was necessary?

10.   How can God's command to be bold in the face of hard circumstances give us strength?

11. Throughout this passage, how is the Lord himself a model of what it means to be a supportive friend?

12. Think of a friend who needs your support during a difficult time. How can you follow the Lord's example in helping that person?

Pray about It

Our Father, like Joshua let us be open to your call on our lives. Your Son, Jesus, said to his eleven disciples, "All authority in heaven and on earth has been given to me. Therefore go and make disciples of all nations, baptizing them in the name of the Father and of the Son and of the Holy Spirit, and teaching them to obey everything I have commanded you. And surely I am with you always, to the very end of the age."

Like your disciples, let us hear and respond to your call on our lives no matter how large or how small. May each of us be strong and courageous, meditating on your Word day and night, remembering always your words, "I will never leave you nor forsake you."

TAKING THE NEXT STEP

"Be bold, be strong, for the Lord your God is with you." If you are going through a difficult time, sit quietly and close your eyes. Take a deep breath, then exhale. Picture God lifting you up and carrying you through this difficulty. With each breath relax your body. God is with you. He will support your weight. He is faithful. (If your life is comfortable now, do this exercise considering a past struggle.)

Consider your friends. Make a list of how each has been supportive to you.

Think of a friend who needs your support. Ask God how you can show support to that friend. List possibilities.

Spend time praising God for his love, faithfulness, and support. Praise God for his promises and requirements and the benefits you experience from both. Thank God for your friends and what they mean to you.

four

HONORING OUR COMMITMENTS

Malachi 2:10–16

I promised a friend that I would care for her three children tonight while she attends a class. I would much prefer to spend the evening with a good book. I have had a very busy day, I am just getting over the flu, and dinner is waiting to be fixed.

Commitments are not always convenient. But God expects us to keep them. When we do, we benefit, others benefit, and God is pleased. In this study we look at a time in Israel when past commitments were not taken seriously and so were disregarded. In turn, Israel feared that God had abandoned his commitment to them. God speaks into this time of cynicism and unbelief to call Israel back to the covenant.

Warming Up

1. Think of a time when someone broke a commitment to you. How did it make you feel?

Digging In

2.   Read Malachi 2:10–16. These verses are full of broken commitments. What specific commitments have been broken?

3.   Consider the three questions posed in verse 10. What point is Malachi trying to make?

4.   Many churches struggle with internal conflicts. How could Malachi's questions help?

5.   What is God's attitude toward Israel's marrying "the daughter of a foreign god" (v. 11)?

6.   Intermarriage with pagans was strictly forbidden because it could lead to apostasy (see Ex. 34:15–16; Deut. 7:3–4). How does this explain Malachi's seemingly harsh prayer in verse 12?

7.   We are influenced by the people with whom we are closest (spouses, friends, business partners, and so on). What can we learn from verses 11 and 12?

8.   The people are confused as to why God does not accept them
      (v. 13). What is the problem (vv. 14–16)?

9.   By observing key words or phrases like *broken faith, partner,* and
      marriage covenant (vv. 14–15), what can we learn about God's view
      of marriage?

10.   How does God's view of marriage help us understand his attitude
      toward divorce (v. 16)?

11. How can knowing God's view of marriage enrich our own marriages? our friendships?

12. Healthy relationships require that we "do not break faith" with those to whom we have committed ourselves (vv. 15–16). How can honoring our commitments make a difference in the way we relate to our spouse or our friends?

Pray about It

Forgive us now, Father, as we humble ourselves before you knowing we are unable to live up to the standards you place before us. Have mercy on us. We're grateful for the work of your son, Jesus Christ, and that through him we are acceptable in your eyes. Flood our hearts with your love and hope. Give us the desire and ability to walk the path you place before us, keeping the faith with you, Father, and with our families and friends.

TAKING THE NEXT STEP

My face is set, my gait is fast, my goal is Heaven, my road is narrow, my way is rough, my companions are few, my guide is reliable, my mission is clear. I cannot be bought, compromised, detoured, lured away, turned back, diluted, or delayed. I will not flinch in the face of sacrifice, hesitate in the presence of adversity, negotiate . . . at the table of the enemy, ponder at the pool of popularity, or meander in a maze of mediocrity. I won't give up, shut up, let up, or slow up.

—Robert Moorhead (*The Book of Positive Quotations*
[Minneapolis: Fairview, 1996])

Consider what God has required of you. What commitments have you made to God? In what ways have you failed God? Yourself?

Healthy relationships require that we do not break faith with those to whom we have committed ourselves. Think of commitments you have made to family or friends. Which ones have you been careless about keeping? What can you do to better honor those commitments?

In quiet, spend time in confession asking God for forgiveness where you have fallen short of your commitments and obligations. Then picture a gentle waterfall flowing into a quiet pool surrounded by green hills. The water is the cleansing, refreshing work of the Holy Spirit. In your mind's eye, stand under the falls, swim in the pool, float, dive, do whatever you wish. This is God's healing space.

five

FULFILLING OUR RESPONSIBILITIES

Matthew 25:14–30

Friendship with others begins with our friendship with God. "You are my friends if you do what I command" (John 15:14). In all relationships there are commitments and obligations. This is especially true in our relationship with God.

In the parable of the talents, Jesus describes his expectations and requirements of his disciples. He calls us to make investments for him, to choose his goals, and then ultimately to "come and share" his happiness. We are called into a relationship of responsibility and friendship.

Warming Up

1. What types of responsibility do you enjoy?

What types of responsibility do you avoid?

Digging In

2.   Read Matthew 25:14–30. As the master leaves on a long journey,
      what resources does he give each of his servants (vv. 14–15)?

What does he expect of his servants?

3. What are some of the resources Jesus has given to you?

        What do you think Jesus expects of you?

4. How does the master show approval to the servants who please him (vv. 21, 23)?

5.   Recall a time when you sensed God's approval. What was it like?

6.   How would you describe the behavior of the wicked servant (vv. 24–30)?

Why do you think the third servant did not invest his master's money?

7.   What image does the third servant have of his master (vv. 24–25)?

How does our image of Jesus affect the way we serve him?

8.   How does the master show his disapproval (vv. 26–30)?

9. The third servant receives a harsh judgment (vv. 28–30). What does Jesus want us to understand about our responsibilities within his kingdom?

10. What investments can you make for the sake of God's kingdom?

11. From this passage, what can we learn about our relationship with Jesus?

How can these principles be applied to our other friendships?

Pray about It

Quietly reflect on this passage, on the Father, Jesus, your responsibilities, and God's joy.

End your reflection time by reading John 15:9–15 and offering the following prayer:

> As the Father has loved me, so have I loved you. Now remain in my love. If you obey my commands, you will remain in my love, just as I have obeyed my Father's commands and remain in his love. I have told you this so that my joy may be in you and that your joy may be complete. My command is this: Love each other as I have loved you. Greater love has no one than this, that he lay down his life for his friends. You are my friends if you do what I command. I no longer call you servants, because a servant does not know his master's business. Instead I have called you friends, for everything that I learned from my Father I have made known to you.

Our Father who is in heaven. Holy is your name. Your kingdom come. Your will be done on earth as it is in heaven. You, Father, are all powerful, and your Son, Jesus, shares in all your glory. We are grateful for the friendship you offer us through Jesus and the responsibilities you give to us. We pray that we may honor you as we invest in your kingdom. Give us wisdom and perseverance as we love and serve you.

TAKING THE NEXT STEP

Referring to the parable of the talents, consider your talents. How is God requiring you to be responsible? What would God like you to invest in his kingdom? Speak to God about your desire to be faithful. Over the next few days, listen. What thoughts and ideas come to mind? Write them down. Then consider how to get started.

Relating this passage to our friendships is difficult because the parable speaks of a master/servant relationship. In our relationships, we do not and should not have the same level of responsibilities and consequences as we do with God; however, friendships do involve responsibilities and obligations. List the responsibilities you believe God has given you regarding a specific friend.

As you consider your investments in God's kingdom and your responsibilities toward a friend, remember you will find the ability to accomplish God's tasks in your relationship to God. Reflect on the following Scripture:

> I am the vine; you are the branches. If a man remains in me and I in him, he will bear much fruit; apart from me you can do nothing. If anyone does not remain in me, he is like a branch that is thrown away and withers; such branches are picked up, thrown into the fire and burned. If you remain in me and my words remain in you, ask whatever you wish, and it will be given you. This is to my Father's glory, that you bear much fruit, showing yourselves to be my disciples.
>
> —John 15:5–8

six

THE REWARDS OF FAITHFULNESS

Proverbs

Very early we discovered that our son Jeremy was motivated by rewards. A five-hour task could be reduced to five minutes if an appropriate reward was offered.

Faithfulness is a lifelong task that requires continual effort. In these proverbs God shows us that there are rich rewards for those who do the hard work:

> Let love and faithfulness never leave you; bind them around your neck, write them on the tablet of your heart. Then you will win favor and a good name in the sight of God and man.
>
> —Proverbs 3:3–4

> Through love and faithfulness sin is atoned for; through the fear of the LORD a man avoids evil.
>
> —Proverbs 16:6

> Love and faithfulness keep a king safe; through love his throne is made secure.
>
> —Proverbs 20:28

> Like a bad tooth or a lame foot is reliance on the unfaithful in times of trouble.
>
> —Proverbs 25:19

Warming Up

1.   What benefits are there in being faithful to a friend?

Digging In

2.   Read the four Proverbs quoted at the beginning of this study. What
       are some of the benefits of faithfulness?

3.   Faithfulness is paired with love in three of the four references. How
       are the two words complementary?

4.   Look at Proverbs 3:3–4. What efforts does it take to gain and keep a good reputation?

5.   What are some of the benefits of a good reputation?

      What are the liabilities of a poor reputation?

6.   Look at Proverbs 16:6. Faithfulness can help us overcome past sins against God and others. How do you think this works in practice?

7.   Fear of the Lord is parallel with faithfulness in this proverb. How are faithfulness and fear of the Lord complementary truths?

8.   How can faithfulness help us to live a godly life?

9.   Look at Proverbs 20:28. Love and faithfulness aren't traditionally hot topics on the political circuit. How would they contribute to a healthy government?

10. How would it affect your attitude toward government to know that your political leaders were seeking to act in love and faithfulness?

11. Look at Proverbs 25:19. How do a bad tooth and a lame foot describe what it is like to depend on an unfaithful person?

12.   We have all had the experience of being let down by someone. How are you affected?

How do you tend to respond?

13.   A life full of faithfulness is a rich life. How do the practical bene-fits of faithfulness motivate you to be a more faithful person to God and to your friends?

Pray about It

Our Father, create in us a heart that desires you. Teach us faithfulness that we may "win favor and a good name" in your sight and before humankind. Teach us to fear you that we may avoid evil and sin. Forgive us for our unfaithful times so that we may begin again fresh and cleansed. May we faithfully walk in your love all the days of our lives.

TAKING THE NEXT STEP

The LORD is my shepherd, I shall not be in want.
He makes me lie down in green pastures,
he leads me beside quiet waters, he restores my soul.
He guides me in paths of righteousness for his name's sake.
Even though I walk through the valley of the shadow of death,
I will fear no evil, for you are with me;
your rod and your staff, they comfort me.
You prepare a table before me in the presence of my enemies.
You anoint my head with oil; my cup overflows.
Surely goodness and love will follow me all the days of my life,
and I will dwell in the house of LORD forever.

—Psalm 23

Psalm 23, written by David, expresses God's faithfulness to David. In it, David is confident that God is involved in every aspect of his life, both good and bad. David sees God as a shepherd, a guide, a protector, a friend. Using your own images and life experiences to express how God has been faithful to you, write your own psalm. Include the names of friends God has brought into your life. Honor God for his faithfulness.

Consider the previous studies and commitments you have made to God and friends. If you have begun to fulfill these commitments, be encouraged and continue on your adventure of faithfulness with God. If not, now is your beginning. Choose one commitment and start today.

LEADER'S NOTES

Leading a Bible discussion—especially for the first time—
can make you feel both nervous and excited. If you are
nervous, realize that you are in good company. Many
biblical leaders, such as Moses, Joshua, and the apostle
Paul, felt nervous and inadequate to lead others (see, for
example, 1 Cor. 2:3). Yet God's grace was sufficient for
them, just as it will be for you.

Some excitement is also natural. Your leadership is a
gift to the others in the group. Keep in mind, however,
that other group members also share responsibility for
the group. Your role is simply to stimulate discussion by
asking questions and encouraging people to respond.
The suggestions listed below can help you to be an effective leader.

PREPARING TO LEAD

1. Ask God to help you understand and apply the passage to your own
   life. Unless that happens, you will not be prepared to lead others.
2. Carefully work through each question in the study guide. Meditate and reflect on the passage as you formulate your answers.
3. Familiarize yourself with the leader's notes for the study. These will
   help you understand the purpose of the study and will provide valu-
   able information about the questions in the study.
4. Pray for the various members of the group. Ask God to use these
   studies to bring about greater spiritual fruit in the life of each
   person.

5. Before the first meeting, make sure each person has a study guide. Encourage them to prepare beforehand for each study.

LEADING THE STUDY

1. Begin the study on time. If people realize that the study begins on schedule, they will work harder to arrive on time.
2. At the beginning of your first time together, explain that these studies are designed to be discussions not lectures. Encourage everyone to participate, but realize that some may be hesitant to speak during the first few sessions.
3. Read the introductory paragraph at the beginning of the discussion. This will orient the group to the passage being studied.
4. Read the passage aloud. You may choose to do this yourself, or you might ask for volunteers.
5. The questions in the guide are designed to be used just as they are written. If you wish, you may simply read each one aloud to the group. Or you may prefer to express them in your own words. However, unnecessary rewording of the questions is not recommended.
6. Don't be afraid of silence. People in the group may need time to think before responding.
7. Avoid answering your own questions. If necessary, rephrase a question until it is clearly understood. Even an eager group will quickly become passive and silent if they think the leader will do most of the talking.
8. Encourage more than one answer to each question. Ask, "What do the rest of you think?" or "Anyone else?" until several people have had a chance to respond.
9. Try to be affirming whenever possible. Let people know you appreciate their insights into the passage.
10. Never reject an answer. If it is clearly wrong, ask, "Which verse led you to that conclusion?" Or let the group handle the problem by asking them what they think about the question.
11. Avoid going off on tangents. If people wander off course, gently bring them back to the passage being considered.

12. Conclude your time together with conversational prayer. Ask God to help you apply those things that you learned in the study.

13. End on time. This will be easier if you control the pace of the discussion by not spending too much time on some questions or too little on others.

Many more suggestions and helps are found in the book *Leading Bible Discussions* (InterVarsity Press). Reading that would be well worth your time.

Study 1

A COMMITMENT TO BE THERE

Ruth 1

Purpose: To discover that faithfulness requires that we stay with a person not only in good times but also in adversity.

The book of Ruth shows us ordinary people who trust in the providence of God as they face painful events in life. The setting is in the days of the Judges, when the faith of Israel is at a low point. The book reflects a time in which there is social unrest, violence, social disintegration, sexual immorality, and war.

Question 1. Every study begins with an "approach question," which is discussed *before* reading the passage. An approach question is designed to do three things.

First, it helps to break the ice. Because an approach question doesn't require any knowledge of the passage or any special preparation, it can get people talking and can help them to warm up to each other.

Second, an approach question can motivate people to study the passage at hand. At the beginning of the study, people in the group aren't necessarily ready to jump into the world of the Bible. Their minds may be on other things (their kids, a problem at work, an upcoming meeting) that have nothing to do with the study. An approach question can capture their interest and draw them into the discussion by raising important issues related to the study. The question becomes a bridge between their personal lives and the answers found in Scripture.

Third, a good approach question can reveal where people's thoughts or feelings need to be transformed by Scripture. That is why it is important to ask the approach question *before* reading the passage. The passage might inhibit the spontaneous, honest answers people might have given, because they feel compelled to give biblical answers. The approach question allows them to compare their personal thoughts and feelings with what they later discover in Scripture.

Question 2. Naomi was left abandoned and hopeless with the death of her husband and sons. In the Old Testament a Hebrew woman was her husband's possession. Although she was more than a slave, she had very few rights, and no inheritance rights. Any position of respect in the community grew out of the male children she bore.

The word translated "widow" communicates loneliness, abandonment, and helplessness. The only hope of recovery of social status for a widow was to marry a second time.

Question 5. Naomi is honest with her feelings. She does not hide her pain, anger, hurt, or belief that God "has gone out against me." The belief that nothing happens by chance permeates the Old Testament. God is sovereign. Whatever happens in one's life is the direct workings of God. Naomi understood God to be judging or punishing her.

Question 6. Depending on the spiritual maturity of the group this question may be answered superficially. It is not easy or "spiritual" to admit that you're angry with God or that you blame him for difficult times. Naomi's example of honesty will be helpful for this discussion question. Owning our emotions, whether they be feelings of anger or love, opens up opportunities for resolution and healing.

Question 7. In observing verses 6 and 7 it is interesting to note that Orpah and Ruth did not question their duty to accompany their mother-in-law, though it meant leaving their own land. Naomi encouraged Ruth and Orpah to stay in Moab because of her devotion and love for them. Naomi didn't want her daughters-in-law to experience life as foreigners in Israel. While God had made provisions in the law for them, aliens were not particularly welcome and were usually excluded from the life of the community. For example, marriage with a Moabite was not forbidden by law (Deut. 7:1, 3), though a Moabite was not allowed in the congregation of the Lord to the tenth generation (Deut. 23:3; Neh. 13:1–3).

In Israel the Levirate Law provided for a childless widow. It was the obligation of a brother to marry his deceased brother's wife. Naomi explains that she has no other sons, nor will she, because she is too old to remarry. Even if she could have sons, she points out to her daughters-in-law that it would be unreasonable (Orpah and Ruth would more than likely be beyond their childbearing years) for them to wait for her sons to reach adulthood. She encourages Orpah and Ruth to return to their mother's house where they will have a better opportunity to remarry and begin a new life.

Question 8. Naomi will be returning to her home of Bethlehem without husband, sons, status, or prospects. Without her daughters-in-law she will face her hopeless situation without the love and companionship of those with whom she has grown intimate through the shared experiences of marriage and death. Yet despite the comfort their companionship brings her, Naomi shows a selfless concern for Orpah and Ruth by releasing them from their obligation to her.

To go with Naomi would mean giving up families, friends, homeland, deities, and prospects for remarriage. Orpah shows her love to Naomi by being obedient to Naomi's wish. She returns to Moab. Ruth shows her love by remaining with Naomi. She sacrifices her own prospects and comforts to accompany Naomi to Bethlehem.

The word *clung* (v. 14) is a verb meaning a committed, faithful "cleaving" in a deep personal relationship.

Question 9. People will be at different levels of loyalty. For one, an expression of loyalty may be visiting a grandfather every six months. For another it may be the twenty-four-hour constant care of a sick grandfather. Both of these situations are valid and should be affirmed. The issue is how God is working in a person's life, not the application of a human standard.

At this point you may also want to ask what cost your loved ones pay in their faithfulness to you.

Question 10. The name Ruth is traditionally derived from *ra'ah*, a word meaning "friend" or "friendship."

In Old Testament times people believed deity had power only in the geographical region occupied by his or her worshipers. Within her declaration of devotion to Naomi, Ruth is proclaiming a commitment to the God of Israel. She is demonstrating a religious or spiritual conversion.

Question 11. In ancient times names often reflected religious beliefs or personality traits. The name Naomi means "pleasant" or "lovely." Yet when Naomi arrives in Bethlehem she declares, "Call me Mara, because the Almighty has made my life very bitter" (Ruth 1:20b). Mara means "bitter." Her return home must have been a shameful experience for her. She, like the rest of the Israelites, believed that God blessed the righteous and brought calamity on the unrighteous (Deut. 28:1–2, 15; Job 11:13–20).

Question 12. Besides the companionship and friendship of Ruth, Naomi has returned home to the people of Israel, the children of God. Even in her humiliation, she will share in the relationships of the community and God's blessing of the barley harvest.

Background material for this study comes from David Atkinson, *The Message of Ruth: The Bible Speaks Today* (Downers Grove, Ill.: InterVarsity), and Frank E. Gaebelein, *The Expositor's Bible Commentary*, vol. 3 (Grand Rapids, Mich.: Zondervan, 1992).

Study 2

A WILLINGNESS TO FORGIVE

Hosea 2:19–3:5

Purpose: To consider how faithfulness seeks forgiveness and reconciliation by looking at God's forgiveness of Israel in the book of Hosea.

The behavior of Gomer is not an indictment of the women of Israel, but of the nation of Israel. All of Israel worshiped the Baals and were therefore guilty of physical and spiritual adultery.

As you study the book of Hosea, it is important to keep in mind that forgiveness is not a given, but is God's free choice. When God grants forgiveness, it is an astounding act of grace.

Question 2. The events in Hosea took place during the reign of Jeroboam II, king of Israel. It was a prosperous time, and Hosea's prophecy of coming judgment must have seemed farfetched. Israel adopted a Canaanite lifestyle, which included worship of their gods. The Baals of the Canaanites were regarded as a source of fertility and prosperity. Orgiastic worship at the shrines was the centerpiece of their religion. In essence, such religion was the opposite of everything embodied in God's covenant.

Question 3. Verses 19–20 focus on the legal and contractual nature of the new relationship. Righteousness and justice were legal standards met in the betrothal. Love and compassion is an expression of God's emotional concern for the bride. "You will acknowledge the Lord" (v. 20) is a statement of Israel's reciprocal faithfulness to God.

In Israelite marriages a betrothal would involve negotiations with the bride's family for a proper bride price, which the suitor would pay. A period of time would pass between the betrothal and the consummation of the relationship, but in that interval the woman was considered to belong officially to her intended and to belong to him for life. The intensity of God's betrothal to Israel is conveyed by repeating *betroth* three times.

Question 4. The worship of the Baals actually involved sexual acts. The relationship between God and his people was one of deep personal intimacy. In the covenant God gave himself to his people and expected no less in return.

Questions 6–7. As a result of the restored mutually faithful relationship, God will "respond." The benefits of forgiveness are more than personal. Verses 21–23 show that the skies (rain) and the earth (crops) become fruitful and productive as God forgives and restores. Likewise, when reconciliation takes place between two people today, the benefits are more than personal. Those around us benefit as well. Encourage group members to think of how this works out in their situations. There can be benefits in attitudes, atmosphere, and even physical health.

Question 8. Hosea is commanded to love Gomer in spite of her unfaithfulness. Likewise, God will restore Israel in spite of her sin.

Question 9. Gomer's sexual promiscuity had evidently settled on one person. Her betrothal price was given to rescue her from financial obligations that bound her to her lover. It is possible that she was "owned" by her lover and was a slave/harlot for him. No payment was officially due because Gomer was still Hosea's wife.

The real cost of restoring Israel (and the church) was paid in the sacrifice of Jesus Christ. In him, once and for all, the betrothal price and cost of redemption from our slavery to sin and Satan was paid in full.

Question 10. Forgiveness is not an easy exercise. It is a matter not of willpower but of surrender, and it may take several levels of surrender. Being willing to forgive is a start, but the actual act of forgiveness may require a time of tending and caring for the wound inflicted. The question, "How have I participated in the drama that has wounded me?" may need an answer. Is forgiveness humanly possible? Sometimes, perhaps; however, God can give us the power and the ability to forgive. Forgiveness is the surrender of ourselves into God's mercy and the gift of mercy to our offender.

Do not allow the group discussion to expound cheap grace. Forgiveness is difficult.

Unforgiveness may cause pain to the person who is not forgiven, but it will definitely cause self-destruction to the reluctant forgiver. It is to our benefit to release our perpetrator from his or her offense.

Background material for this study comes from David Allan Hubbard, *Hosea, The Tyndale Old Testament Commentaries* (Downers Grove, Ill.: InterVarsity Press, 1989), and Frank E. Gaebelein, *The Expositor's Bible Commentary*, vol. 3 (Grand Rapids, Mich.: Zondervan, 1992).

Study 3

A PROMISE OF SUPPORT

Joshua 1:1–9

Purpose: To realize that personal support is an important facet of faithfulness.

Question 2. Moses had an astounding relationship with God that shaped the nation forever after. His closeness to God was glimpsed when he met God face to face on the mountain top and received the Ten Commandments.

Under his leadership there were numerous miracles, such as parting the Red Sea, water gushing from a rock, and manna and quail for food. And there were the judgments by God: destroying the golden calf, snakebites, restrictions on entering the land, and so on.

Moses' accomplishments included writing the Pentateuch and administering the Law by organizing judges of tens, hundreds, and thousands. He also set up religious worship, including the tabernacle and the Levitical priesthood.

It would be difficult to overestimate the importance of Moses to Israel, but remember that Joshua was Moses' assistant. He saw Moses during his ordinary times. Joshua observed Moses' weaknesses, his stuttering, his temper, his disobedience, and his discouragements, as well as his great moments.

Question 3. Observe that God not only promises his presence (a promise not to be taken lightly) but also assures Joshua that there will be no successful resistance to him as long as he lives. The fact that this was the land promised to Moses and Israel's forefathers would also have been an encouragement. The land God would lead Israel into had been identified, chosen, and set aside.

Question 4. The secret of Moses' success had been God's presence with him. The secret to Joshua's success would also be God's presence.

Question 6. God requires of Joshua strength, courage, obedience to all the law, and meditation on the law day and night. The words "do not turn from it [the law] to the right or to the left" (v. 7) communicate that there must be no deviation. The phrase "from your mouth" (v. 8) refers to the custom of muttering while reflecting or studying. When constantly muttering the law of God, Joshua would definitely be thinking about it.

Question 7. Meditating on the law would keep Joshua's focus on God as he took on the task of establishing the nation of Israel in the Promised Land.

Question 10. God presents strength and courage as a choice, a decision. It is a way of standing, of positioning oneself. Just as taking special care of one's outward appearance helps create an inner confidence, this command to be strong and have courage may encourage similar results.

Question 11. God communicates to Joshua both support and conditions. His love is faithful. His promise of support is reliable, but he requires individual responsibility. The question may arise, "Are we to give unconditional support to a friend?" While a friend should be there to support and encourage, he or she must not enable a person's addiction or encourage a codependent relationship. Our love is to be unconditional, while our support and the actions we take may need adjustment depending on the friend's situation.

Background material for this study comes from Frank E. Gaebelein, *The Expositor's Bible Commentary*, vol. 3 (Grand Rapids, Mich.: Zondervan Publishing House, 1992).

Study 4

HONORING OUR COMMITMENTS

Malachi 2:10–16

Purpose: To learn how important it is to remain faithful to God in our commitments.

Background: Malachi was written in a "silent" time. The Jews returned from their Babylonian exile with high hopes. They rebuilt the temple and the walls of Jerusalem. As the years passed, however, they became disillusioned as the expected prosperity of their country did not come. They were surrounded by enemies, and they suffered drought, bad crops, and famine. They began to doubt God's love. They saw their enemies as being blessed and began to think that there was no profit in obedience. They became cynical, unbelieving, and gave up obedience to the law.

This is a study of commitments or, more accurately, the breaking of commitments, particularly in the areas of religion, marriage, and divorce. Be sensitive as you lead the study. It is not intended to create an abundance of guilt. The study does, however, look at God's standards for marriage, and not all of us have been able to live up to them. (All of us have failed to live up to them inwardly.) It is important to remember that the questions and concerns raised in the study should drive us to God and his mercy rather than into despair.

Question 2. In verse 10 when Malachi speaks about "breaking faith with one another," he is most likely speaking of all betrayals among the Israelites, from simple unkindness to gross injustices. More specifically, in verses 11 and 12 he speaks about marrying foreigners, and in verses 14–16 he speaks about betrayal in marriage and divorce.

Question 3. Israel is bound together by a common God, with common ancestors, and the covenant given at Mount Sinai. Malachi sees these things as the foundation of their national existence. They should bind Israel together in a community of justice and faithfulness. Malachi considers it intolerable that this unity is being broken by their sin. The essence communicated by these questions is that the Israelites should cooperate with each other, work harmoniously together, and marry within their own nation.

The word *Father* is ambiguous. The NIV, by capitalizing the word, seems to imply that it refers to God. It is more probable that it refers to one of the patriarchs, as there is no precedent in the Old Testament for referring to God as Father in the manner that Jesus taught Christians to do. The word *father* probably refers to Jacob, since Malachi refers to Jacob in 1:2; 2:12; and 3:6.

Question 5. Marrying outside of the Israelite nation created for the Jew the real possibility of compromise of his religious fervor and practice. Paul also speaks about this in a Christian context in 2 Corinthians 6:14–17: "Do not be yoked together with unbelievers. For what do righteousness and wickedness have common? Or what fellowship can light have with darkness? What harmony is there between Christ and Belial? What does a believer have in common with an unbeliever? What agreement is there between the temple of God and idols? For we are the temple of the living God. As God has said: 'I will live with them and walk among them, and I will be their God, and they will be my people. Therefore come out from them and be separate,' says the Lord. . . . 'I will be a Father to you, and you will be my sons and daughters, says the Lord Almighty.'"

In verse 11 the phrase "the daughter of a foreign god" may also literally be translated "adopt a pagan religion."

Question 6. The phrase "to be cut off from the tents of Jacob" implies that the offender is excluded from the community of Israel. The offender's sacrifice to the Lord is unacceptable because by the act of intermarriage he has chosen disobedience as a way of life.

The Lord's objection to intermarriage is religious, not racial.

Question 8. There are two issues to be aware of here. One is that the people are distressed because of the lack of divine acceptance of their offerings and the absence of God's blessings on their lives. However, they are not bemoaning or distressed about their sin. The second issue is, of course, that of men being unfaithful to their wives. The phrase "wife of your youth" (v. 14) suggests that men are divorcing aging wives for younger women.

Question 9. Malachi emphasizes marriage as a partnership. The Hebrew word for *partnership* is often used in the masculine to refer to a close friend with whom one shares interests, whether good or bad. In this text it refers to the wife.

Israelites saw marriage as a covenant to which the Lord was a witness. This should have contributed to the couple's stability and loyalty as partners.

Verse 15 says that God made marriages monogamous and intended for them to last. The Hebrew underlying verse 15 is not clear. Therefore each translation contains an interpretation. The general understanding is that because of the unity between husband and wife, the rearing of children is a shared responsibility. In an atmosphere of love and stability, children can be nurtured by godly principles. Family relationships are to illustrate love and loyalty and should embody the divine covenant between God and Israel.

Question 10. Be sensitive here. There are probably people in your study who have gone through a divorce. (Perhaps even yourself.) We shouldn't avoid looking at God's standards, because grace and forgiveness are available to those who come to him.

The phrase "I hate a man's covering himself with violence as well as with his garment" (v. 16) is a figurative expression that means "I hate all kinds of gross injustice."

Background material for this study comes from *The New Bible Commentary: Revised* (Grand Rapids, Mich.: Eerdmans, 1970), Joyce G. Baldwin, *Haggai, Zechariah, Malachi, Tyndale Old Testament Commentaries* (Downers Grove, Ill.: InterVarsity, 1972), and Frank E. Gaebelein, *The Expositor's Bible Commentary*, vol. 7 (Grand Rapids, Mich.: Zondervan, 1992).

Study 5

FULFILLING OUR RESPONSIBILITIES

Matthew 25:14–30

Purpose: To consider the importance of faithfully fulfilling our responsibilities until Jesus returns.

This parable reveals events of the "settled accounts" when God's kingdom is consummated. The fate of the worthless servant is serious and a good warning. However, for those who easily lose confidence, relentless guilt is not a good response to this study. Until the final judgment, a believer's dark or joyless times are opportunities to draw closer to God. Remember that the purpose of this study is to consider the importance of faithfully fulfilling our responsibilities until Jesus returns.

Question 2. The introduction to the parable of the talents seems abrupt. This indicates that it is closely tied to the previous parable and shares its introduction: "At that time the kingdom of heaven will be like. . . ."

The word *talent* means money, a unit of exchange. It could have been referring to gold, silver, or copper. The worth of a talent is difficult to calculate; however, it can be assumed that the parable is dealing with large sums of money.

During this time period, slaves and servants experienced considerable responsibility and authority. The master in this parable was giving his servants responsibility for his cash assets. It appears that he is making them partners in his affairs, partners who share his profits. It is important to note that the master distributes the talents according to his evaluation of his servants' capacities.

In verses 16–18 the phrase "and put his money to work" does not necessarily imply investing the money in a lending agency. It is more likely that the servant set up a business and worked to increase the capital. The third servant appears to be unwilling to work or even take the risk of depositing his master's money. (During this time period deposit systems were not particularly safe.)

Question 3. The talent can be used to symbolize various applications and possibilities, including money. Many see the talents in this passage as living up to our full potential. This is incorrect. The talents should not be seen as natural endowments given to people in general, but as specific privileges and opportunities to invest in the kingdom of heaven.

It is worth considering gifts of the Spirit as well as fruits of the Spirit (love, peace, joy, faithfulness, and so on) as some of the resources that Jesus has given to us to invest in his kingdom.

Question 4. In verse 19 the phrase "after a long time" is referring to the long delay of the consummation of the kingdom. As in the parable of the ten virgins, the servants must be watchful, resourceful, and persevering. The two servants who have been responsible with their master's wealth both receive verbal affirmation, increased responsibilities, and a share of their master's joy; however, they do not receive increased responsibility in equal amounts. The point of this parable is not egalitarianism, but the increase of responsibility and a share of the master's joy according to the ability of each. There is an emphasis in this parable of "to whom much is given, from him also shall much be required."

Question 6. Because of the third servant's understanding of who his master is, he is unwilling to accept his responsibilities and obligations. Perhaps the servant believes that if he invested the money entrusted to him, he (the servant) would see too little of the profit or that if he failed, he would experience the master's wrath. Perhaps the servant was insulted at receiving less than the other two servants. Was the burial of the money a spiteful act? The servant's irresponsible action betrays his lack of love for his master. In the end, the wicked servant blames his master for the failure and excuses himself. The master exposes this servant as wicked and lazy. The message here is that even those who are given less are obligated to use and develop what they have. The third servant represents a discipleship of achieving nothing. Being faithful involves active, responsible service.

Question 7. The servant sees his master as hard, grasping and exploiting the labors of others. The master answers him in such a way as to show how distorted the wicked servant's thinking is and uses the servant's own words to condemn him. If, in fact, the master is so harsh, then the wicked servant should have been very careful to make investments with the money given him.

Question 9. We are accountable to the Master for our actions and investments. Failure to be responsible with the investments of the kingdom carries with it the penalty of having those investments withdrawn and being given no invitation to enter into the joy of the Lord. The servant is destined to stay in darkness.

Question 11. Take this opportunity to now refocus on the positive aspects of our relationship to Jesus. Jesus sees us as more than his servants. He sees us as partners in whom he entrusts his riches and in whom he shares the profits and rewards of his kingdom. Jesus does not require more from us than we are able to do. He distributes the talents to "each according to his ability." In our relationship with God we are called to be faithful and responsible. If we are faithful and responsible, we are more than servants and partners. We are friends.

In John 15:9–15 Jesus speaks to his disciples about their relationship to him and the Father: "As the Father has loved me, so have I loved you. Now remain in my love. If you obey my commands, you will remain in my love, just as I have obeyed my Father's commands and remain in his love. I have told you this so that my joy may be in you and that your joy may be complete. My command is this: Love each other as I have loved you. Greater love has no one than this, that he lay down his life for his friends. You are my friends if you do what I command. I no longer call you servants, because a servant does not know his master's business. Instead I have called you friends, for everything that I learned from my Father I have made known to you."

Resources for the Gospel of Matthew include Richard France, *Matthew,* Tyndale New Testament Commentaries (Grand Rapids, Mich.: Eerdmans, 1987), R. V. G. Tasker, *The Gospel of Matthew,* Tyndale New Testament Commentaries (Grand Rapids, Mich.: Eerdmans, 1961), and Frank E. Gaebelein, *The Expositor's Bible Commentary,* vol. 8 (Grand Rapids, Mich.: Zondervan, 1992).

Study 6

THE REWARDS OF FAITHFULNESS

Proverbs 3:3–4; 16:6; 20:28; 25:19

Purpose: To encourage people to pursue a life of faithfulness by learning that the faithful are rewarded and that unfaithful people cannot be trusted.

Faithfulness in the Old Testament involved keeping the covenant between God and his people. God promised to take Israel as his people and to be their God. In return, Israel promised to worship God and to keep his law.

The word *faithful* can also be translated as "true." The central idea is that one who is faithful and conforms to the standard of God's law is therefore straight and true, not crooked, bent, or falling short.

Question 3. The key to interpreting a proverb is to pay attention to the parallel words and phrases. The two words or phrases often carry the same idea but from a different angle. By comparing the two, their meaning is enriched and deepened.

Also, as in this case, the two words can be used as a hendiadys. A hendiadys is a figure of speech in which two words connected by a conjunction are used to express a single notion that would normally be expressed by an adjective and a substantive, such as *grace and favor* instead of *gracious favor* (*The American Heritage Dictionary of the English Language*, 3d ed.). In this case *love and faithfulness* could be combined as *faithful love*.

Love (Hebrew: *hesed*) can also be translated as "loyalty" and "trustworthiness." *Hesed* is a word that is hard to understand apart from the idea of the covenant. It represents covenant love. The full range of this meaning is found in Matthew 22:37–40: "'Love the Lord your God with all your heart and with all your soul and with all your mind.' This is the first and greatest commandment. And the second is like it: 'Love your neighbor as yourself.' All the Law and the Prophets hang on these two commandments."

Faithfulness (Hebrew: *met*) means "firmness, trustworthiness, stability." Faithfulness requires reality and truth.

Question 4. To "bind" the qualities of love and faithfulness "around your neck" is a constant reminder of God's requirements. But we are required to do more than remember. We are to "write them on the tablet of [our] heart." These qualities are to become part of the disciple's nature.

A life characterized by faithfulness does not come easily; it requires determination. We must choose to be faithful every day and in each situation. The outcome is favor and good repute. This may mean that the practice of love and faithfulness will bring about not only divine and human favor, but divine and human recognition. Luke 2:52 states, "And Jesus grew in wisdom and stature, and in favor with God and men."

Question 6. This verse uses synonymous parallelism. The first half speaks of atonement for sin and the second half avoidance of sin. The emphasis is on complete freedom from sin. It suggests that love and faithfulness bring atonement for sin, but this is not stated as a formal principal of atonement. It expresses God's basic requirements under the covenant with Israel (Mic. 6:6–8). Perhaps God's divine anger against our sin is turned away. Practically speaking, if we are faithful and loving toward those we have hurt and offended, it is possible that we can make restitution.

Question 7. In this verse love and faithfulness are paralleled to the fear of the Lord. It communicates that there will be a departure from evildoing and sin out of a reverent awe of God. In *Roget's Super Thesaurus* Henry Link is quoted as saying that fear is "nature's warning signal to get busy." Henry Ward Beecher says fear is "the soul's signal for rallying." Fear is "a slinking cat I find beneath the lilacs of my mind," states Sophie Tunnel. Fear can be the understanding of the powerful magnificence of God. And knowing God's power can be as motivating to live a faithful life as knowing his love.

Question 8. *Roget's Super Thesaurus* gives the following list as synonyms to the word *faithful*: loyal, true, true-blue, trustworthy, devoted, allegiant, steadfast, staunch, patriotic, tried and true, honorable, *semper fidelis*. When one aspires to faithfulness, their focus becomes the one in whom their faithfulness is placed. A person will "bind" the qualities of love and faithfulness "around [their] neck" and "write them on the tablet of [their] heart." With this type of devotion, how can one not live a godly life?

Questions 9–10. This proverb again refers to the covenant. The idea here is that faithful covenant love brings stability to society. "In the Davidic covenant (2 Sam. 7:11–16) God promised not to take his covenant love (*hesed*) from the king (v. 15) but to make his house stable ('will endure,' v. 16)" (*The Expositors Bible Commentary*). It is God and his faithfulness that makes the land secure. However, divine protection requires the king to rule with loyalty to the covenant. Loyalty and faithfulness are the marks of an ideal king. The covenant mercy of God upholds his throne.

Question 11. An unfaithful person is like a bad tooth or a lame foot. Each is painful and ineffective. This proverb points out that an unfaithful person is useless and that placing your trust in an unfaithful person during a troubled time is pointless. He or she can be of no help.

Background material for this study comes from *The New Bible Commentary: Revised* (Grand Rapids, Mich.: Eerdmans, 1970), or Frank E. Gaebelein, *The Expositor's Bible Commentary*, vol. 5 (Grand Rapids, Mich.: Zondervan, 1992).

BE SURE TO CHECK THESE OTHER GREAT BIBLE STUDY SERIES GUIDES!

New Community:
This series creates an opportunity for a small group to study the Bible in-depth, as it builds community. Each study probes Scripture in a way that strengthens bonds and relationships.

Tough Questions:
This set of guides creates a nonthreatening opportunity to examine the difficult and challenging questions non-Christians ask about the Christian faith.

Pursuing Spiritual Transformation:
These guides explore fresh, biblically based ways to think about and experience your life with God.

InterActions:
This small group discussion guide challenges a deeper level of sharing and application of Scripture in everyday experiences.

Women of Faith:
Designed especially for women to help them develop lives of friendship, joy, faith, and prayer, Women of Faith study guides bring laughter and encouragement to your interaction.

Knowing God:
Develop intimacy with God by discovering his attributes, his love for his children, and his power to change lives.

The Discipleship Series:
This series is designed to make stronger and more effective disciples of Jesus Christ. Eight study guides introduce key aspects of true Christ-followers: *Basic Beliefs, Building Character, Knowing Scripture, New Life in Christ, Sharing Your Faith, Spiritual Disciplines,* and *Spiritual Warfare.*

Walking with God:
This best-selling 6-book series takes an in-depth look at your relationship with God and your action as a member of his kingdom. Two 500-page leader's guides, each supporting three study guides, ensure thoughtful, informative discussions.

The Great Books of the Bible:
This study series leads you through a collection of eight foundational and favorite books of the Bible, including *Ephesians, James, John, Philippians, Proverbs, Psalms, Revelation,* and *Romans.*

Living Encounters:
These guide you on a journey to faith at the cutting edge. Prepare to meet Jesus in ways that will expand your paradigm of Christianity, liberate your spiritual passion, and fill you with joy and spiritual vigor.

Visit www.BibleStudyGuides.com for more information.

Zondervan *Groupware*™

Discover the most effective tools available for your teaching ministry

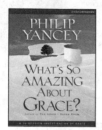 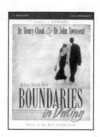  

Zondervan*Groupware* consists of curriculum packages developed with the assistance of experts and based on education research. Each resource simplifies the leader's role by giving them an easy to use Leader's Guide and bringing in experts and examples on brief video segments. Individual Participant's Guides complete everything you need to help your church members experience dynamic personal spiritual growth in a group setting of any size.

Zondervan*Groupware* delivers personal spiritual growth through:

- **Compelling biblical content**

- **Minimal preparation time** for both leader and participant

- **Proven learning techniques** using individual participant's guides and a variety of media

- **Meaningful interaction** in groups of any size, in any setting

- **Emphasis on life application**

Church leaders depend on Zondervan*Groupware* for the best and most accessible teaching material that emphasizes interaction and discussion within group learning situations. Whether a Sunday school class, midweek gathering, Bible study, or other small group setting, Zondervan*Groupware* offers video segments as catalysts to teaching, discussing, understanding, and applying biblical truth. Zondervan*Groupware* provides you with everything you need to effectively incite personal spiritual growth through interpersonal relationships.

Visit www.BibleStudyGuides.com for a complete list of
Zondervan*Groupware* products.

The Fruit of the Spirit Bible

A ONE-YEAR STUDY FOR CULTIVATING A FRUITFUL LIFE

The Fruit of the Spirit Bible is designed with one goal in mind: to help you become more like Jesus—so much like him that your family, friends, and others in your life can see him reflected in your words, attitudes, and actions. *The Fruit of the Spirit Bible* features:

- 52 one-week journeys into becoming like Jesus. With reference to a specific Bible passage and an inspiring note on one of the nine fruit of the Spirit, each "home page" serves as a springboard to further reflections for the next four days of study.

NIV – Most Read.
Most Trusted.

- Over 500 textual inserts explore Scripture passages on the fruit of the Spirit in an interesting and sometimes paradoxical way.
- 36 character profiles uncover lessons on the fruit of the Spirit from the lives of men and women of the Bible.
- Side-column reference system helps you to expand your study.
- Topical index helps you to conduct swift, effective studies on select subjects.
- Concordance helps you quickly locate key passages.

NIV Translation   Size 6 x 9
Most Read. Most Trusted.
Hardcover 0-310-91807-3
Softcover 0-310-91808-1

The Fruit of the Spirit

BECOMING THE PERSON GOD WANTS YOU TO BE

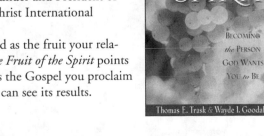

Thomas E. Trask and Wayde I. Goodall
Foreword by Bill Bright, Founder and President of
Campus Crusade for Christ International

Your witness for Christ is as good as the fruit your relationship with him produces. *The Fruit of the Spirit* points you toward a lifestyle that makes the Gospel you proclaim attractive to others because they can see its results.

Softcover 0-310-22787-9

ZONDERVAN™

We want to hear from you. Please send your comments about this
book to us in care of the address below. Thank you.

GRAND RAPIDS, MICHIGAN 49530
w w w . z o n d e r v a n . c o m